BOB'S POT

by Mary Beth Spann

Bob has a pot.

Bob has a box.

Bob drops a lot in the pot.
Kerplop!

Bob puts on the top.

The pot gets hot.

Hot! Hot! Hot!

The popcorn starts to pop.

Pop! Pop! Pop!

Oh, no! The popping will not
stop. Spot licks his chops.

Pop! Pop! Pop!

Flip flop—off goes the top!

Bob stops the pot.

Bob gets a mop.

Spot likes popcorn a lot.

Oh no! Spot's going to pop!